mouths making water

a stage adaption of
james joyce's finnegans wake

by marc-ivan o'gorman

Title: Mouths Making Water

A Dramatisation of James Joyce's "Finnegans Wake"

Author: Marc-Ivan O'Gorman

Release Date: June 2018 [EBook 978-1-925723-02-1]

Language: English

ISBN 978-1-925723-01-4

Illustrations by Anthony Walsh

Cover design by Aiden Grenelle

Book design by Richard O'Gorman

Original production Cleverality Productions
bit.ly/Cleverality

Original soundtrack by Spinning Boy
https://thespinningboy.bandcamp.com/album/mouths-making-water

Published by Apostrophe Press 2018

www.apostrophe.press

foreword

James Joyce spent nearly 20 years writing, and rewriting, his final novel; more than 600 pages of densely written, multi-layered, cryptic text. Having completed the most celebrated novel of all time, *Ulysses*, in 1922, he would devote his remaining years to creating, what was originally entitled '*Work-in-Progress*', but what we know today as, *Finnegans Wake*.

As an Irishman, I felt it was my duty to read everything written by my compatriot, a cultural icon and giant of literature. From *Dubliners*, to *Portrait of the Artist as a Young Man*, to *Ulysses*, his modernist style becomes increasingly ludic and complex, yet I found his work accessible, lyrical and touching. But *Finnegans Wake* was of a different order, it left me flummoxed.

In February 2015, when I was commissioned to direct a play of my choice for a group of Irish acting students as their graduate performance piece, I realised there was a rare opportunity for everyone involved to truly test their mettle. By deciding to adapt *Finnegans Wake*, and challenging the students to perform it, I would be compelled to revisit Joyce's magnum opus, and to fully digest it, in order to put it on the stage, while the students would be called upon to deliver the most difficult text of their lives.

In the beginning was the word. *Finnegans Wake* strives to capture Logos, to describe the history of story. In this "gigantic wheeling rebus", Joyce conjures up a textual primordial soup, the source of all characters and all narratives. In the performance I wanted to embody the atavistic qualities of the writing. The show would be a ritualistic piece, a recounting of a creation myth from some ancient sacred text. Light would be brought up on a murky and barren stage, and antediluvian figures would emerge. The audience could not use reason alone to process what they were party to, they needed to be immersed in the work, the show would wash over them.

This is where we get the title MOUTHS MAKING WATER, for it is only through speaking the words aloud, that we can, as Joyce himself suggested, truly understand this mellifluous book. Joyce was a lifelong music fan and his last book was the most euphonic of all his writing. Not only does it drift the furthest from a literary form towards a musical one, but the sentences themselves sing from the page. In many ways, MOUTHS MAKING WATER is closer to opera than to theatre. The title also plays upon the most widely known fact about the *Wake*, that it contains the names of at least a thousand rivers and other bodies of water. In all cultures water is central to the symbolic narrative of how the world began, whether its Egypt's emergence from the chaotic waters of Nun, Hinduism's Vaivasvata, the progenitor of Man, saved from the great flood, Yu forging China from the cataclysmic overflow of the Yellow River, or indeed, the Biblical deluge. Civilization in its embryonic form floats in the amniotic fluid of legend. So the proto-story is the tale of water, and consequently, the water cycle, or loop, features as a key image in the show. Here we have the never-ending story, the cycle of life, and, Joyce's recurring obsession, the transmigration of souls: reincarnation.

The first question to be asked of any text when attempting to transform it into a dramatic work is: "are there any characters?" Fortunately, in *Finnegans Wake* there are, but like everything else in the book, we are spoilt for choice, thousands are named. The great mythologist, Joseph Campbell, who popularized Joyce's Wakean neologism, *monomyth*, to describe the universal story - suggesting that all stories have essentially the same structure - explains in, *A Skeleton Key to Finnegans Wake*, the first exegesis of the work, that Joyce was attempting to construct his own cyclical, meta-narrative, a story about every story. It follows then, that the characters involved would represent everybody, and that is exactly what we get. The book's main character, arguably, is a chap by the name of Here Comes Everybody, aka HCE, aka Humphrey Chimpden Earwicker, the titular head of a somewhat dysfunctional Dublin family.

Just as the narrative is protean, so too are the characters in *Finnegans Wake*, they are constantly evolving avatars, fluid jungian archetypes, or in Campbell's terms, heroes of a thousand faces. While this is feasible, even desirable, in a novel, in order to stage a text one must choose an interpretation, actual corporeal individuals must embody definable dramatis personae, and in MOUTHS MAKING WATER they are as follows; HCE, a pub owner from Chapelizod, his daughter, Izzy, and his wife Anna Livia Plurabelle. HCE has disgraced himself through some obscene act in the Phoenix Park, the large urban park in Dublin City, and Izzy berates him about it. Anna Livia remains distant and aloof from such carnal indiscretions, she bemoans her absent children, they have abandoned her in her old age and she reminisces about her youth, a youth she sees blossoming, in all its effulgence, in Izzy. There are two young men. Twin brothers. They are both versions of HCE and, at the same time his sons, and the authors of the story; Shem the Penman and Shaun the Postman. Shem is James Joyce, the dissolute artist, a shambling poet; untrustworthy, irresponsible and degenerate. He accepts all criticism, as he fully acknowledges his wasted life of letters. Shaun is also James Joyce, the public face, he is prideful, judgmental and businesslike. Where Shem writes the letter, Shaun delivers it. And then there are the washerwomen, Miss Doddpebble and Missus Quickenough, two characters reminiscent of Shakespearean servants, colourfully commenting on the main action. Joyce described the opening section of the book as "a chattering dialogue across the river by two washerwomen who, as night falls, become a tree and a stone." These are our seven characters.

If *Ulysses*, a virtuosic display of the modernist writing techniques, forming a heady mixture of stream-of-consciousness, classical allusion and secular catechism, is a study of the day (one day in particular: 16th June 1904), then *Finnegans Wake*, as a contemporary reviewer described it, in using "language as a new medium, breaking down all grammatical usages, all time space values, all ordinary conceptions of context." is a study of the Night. A tenebrous, dream-like world where dimly perceived stories conflate. A priority of MOUTHS MAKING WATER, is to convey, through performance, sound design and lighting, this phantasmagorical experience, or to present, as Joyce describes it, his attempts to "reconstruct the nocturnal life" and to "experiment in interpreting 'the dark night of the soul'.

Though there are numerous themes within the novel, including explorations of Irish history, Celtic and Greek mythology, the Old Testament, the fall of man, and Catholic ideas of guilt, sex and Original Sin, the dominant theme in MOUTHS MAKING WATER is the water cycle. The epic novel starts mid sentence describing the flow of the Liffey; "a way a lone a last a loved a long the riverrun, past Eve and Adam's, from swerve of shore to bend of bay, brings us by a commodius vicus of recirculation back to Howth Castle and Environs", and ends midway through the same sentence. We begin with the gossiping washerwomen plying their trade on the banks of the river and end correspondingly with Anna Livia's valediction, a monologue, incidentally, which carries resonances with Molly Bloom's at the end of Ulysses.

Performed in the round, with the washerwomen describing a circle of wet rags on the perimeter of the stage, and the characters moving in diametric pairs, orbiting the central figure of Anna Livia, the fluvial mother, visually expresses the cyclical motif at the heart of the work. Anna Livia's speech, while cataloging rivers from around the globe, is accompanied by a soundtrack of original music, specifically composed for the production, consisting of audio loops, at the same time, discrete portions of her lines are electronically sampled and repeated. Whether reflecting Campbell's universal heroic cycle, the circadian rhythms of sleep, or Christian and eastern philosophical concepts of death and rebirth, MOUTHS MAKING WATER portrayed the literal sense of revolution in *Finnegans Wake*.

Ultimately, the goal is to make some sense of the text and present it in a manner that makes Joyce's book comprehensible to the uninitiated, to present a primer of a deeply complex and rewarding novel. Recognising that Joyce was an acclaimed singer, a musical aficionado, and, by the time he crafted his final words, practically blind, and therefore writing primarily for the ear, suggested that privileging the role of rhythm and sound in the language is the key to performing *Finnegans Wake*. As a review of the first production described MOUTHS MAKING WATER: "Rather than try to make Joyce's impenetrable text accessible for simple meaning, the actors performed the lines as poetry, accentuating the musicality and hidden emotion of the book. The effect was quite hypnotic. The disciplined ensemble movement and use of sound added to the sense of a dense voice poem coming vividly to life in an entrancing theatrical ritual."

It has been one of the great pleasures of my creative life to interpret this literary genius's last work, and I am delighted to invite you to sample a morsel of it, if only to whet your appetite for the main course. Enjoy, and remember "every telling has a taling and that's the he and the she of it".

Marc-Ivan O'Gorman

the play: mouths making water

A performance in 70 minutes with no interval.

characters

- **humphrey chimpden earwicker (hce)**
  A disgraced Dublin bar owner, man.

- **anna livia plurabelle**
  HCE's wife, the river Liffey, mother earth, the eternal life force.

- **shem the penman**
  Anna & HCE's son, a dissolute poet, a disgrace and aware of it.

- **shaun the postman**
  Shem's twin brother, the presentable alternative, the judgmental one.

- **izzy earwhicker**
  Their sister, an outspoken, indignant daughter and the future Anna Livia.

- **miss doddpebble**
  A young, inquiring, gossipy washerwoman who turns into a stone.

- **missus quickenough**
  An old, know-it-all, gossipy washerwoman who turns into an elm.

costumes

- humphrey chimpden earwicker (hce)

• anna livia plurabelle

• shaun the postman

shem the penman

miss doddpebble

missus quickenough

• izzy earwhicker

xvi

floorplan

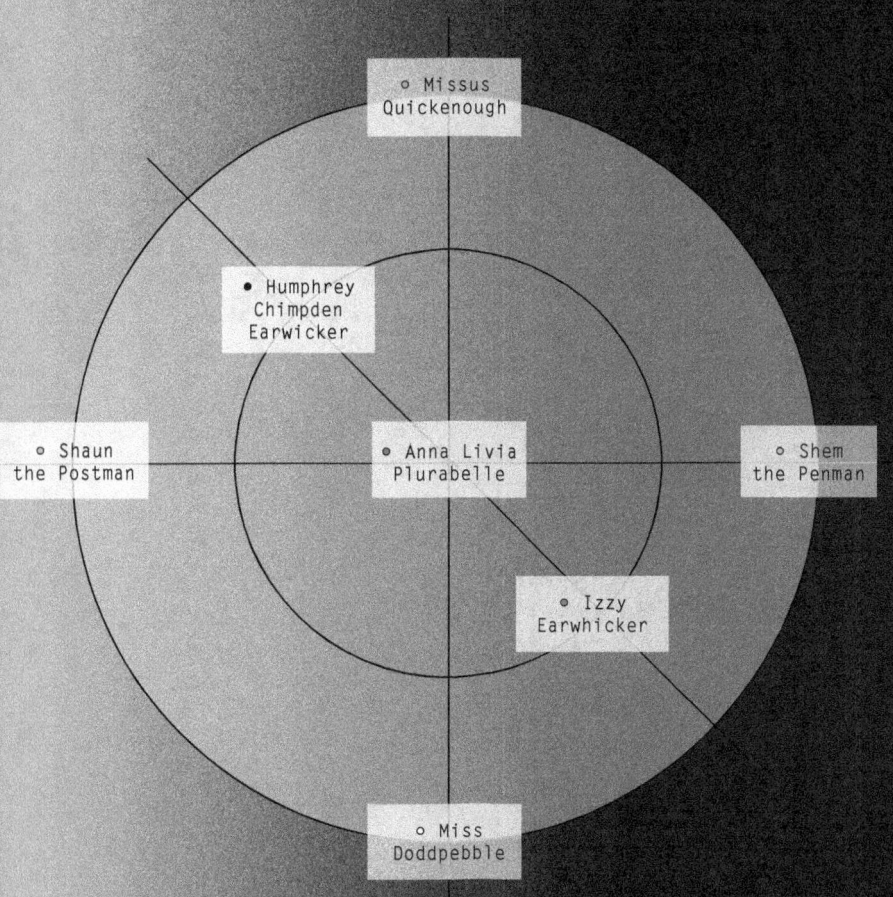

scenes

scene 1 — page 3
A young (Miss Doddpebble) and Old (Missus Quickenough) Washer Women gossip about Anna Livia as they wash clothes on the side of the Liffey.

scene 2 — page 9
Anna Livia reminisces about her life and welcomes the idea of her daughter taking over her mantel.

scene 3 — page 13
Izzy (Anna's daughter) puts to her father (H.C.E.) the rumours about him performing some inappropriate act in the park. He initially denies, but then ultimately admits his guilt.

scene 4 — page 19
Shaun outlines how and Why his twin brother Shem is a total loser and a fake. Shem accepts all of it.

scene 5 — page 23
Washer women continue their gossip about Anna Livia and her family.

scene 6 page 27
> Shaun outlines how and why his twin brother Shem is a total loser based on the rubbish food and drink he enjoys.

scene 7 page 31
> Washer women continue their gossip about Anna Livia and her family.

scene 8 page 35
> Anna Livia arrives to protect her favorite son Shem from his bullying brother.

scene 9 page 39
> Following his public shaming H.C.E. has hit the bottle and is drunkenly reminiscing about the good old days.

scene 10 page 47
> Anna Livia bids farewell to the world as she merges with the Ocean.

scene 11 page 49
> Night falls and washer women slowly turn into a stone and an elm.

mouths making water

scene 1

- miss doddpebble
    O tell me all about Anna Livia!
    I want to hear all about Anna Livia.

- missus quickenough
    Well, you know Anna Livia?

- miss doddpebble
    Yes, of course, we all know Anna
    Livia. Tell me all. Tell me now.

- missus quickenough
    You'll die when you hear. Well, you know, when
    the old cheb went futt and did what you know.

- miss doddpebble
    Yes, I know, go on.

- missus quickenough
    Wash quit and don't be dabbling. Tuck up
    your sleeves and loosen your talk-tapes. And
    don't butt me – hike! – when you bend. Or
    what – ever it was they threed to make out
    he thried to two in the Fiendish park. He's
    an awful old reppe. Look at the shirt of him!
    Look at the dirt of it! He has all my water

black on me. And it steeping and stuping
since this time last wik. How many goes
is it I wonder I washed it? I know by heart
the places he likes to saale, duddurty devil!
Scorching my hand and starving my famine to
make his private linen public. Wallop it well
with your battle and clean it. My wrists are
wrusty rubbing the mouldaw stains. And the
dneepers of wet and the gangres of sin in it!

- miss doddpebble

What was it he did a tail at all on
Animal Sendai? And how long was
he under loch and neagh?

- missus quickenough

It was put in the newses what he did, nicies
and priers, the King fierceas Humphrey, with
illysus dis-tilling, exploits and all. But toms will
till. I know he well. Temp untamed will hist
for no man. As you spring so shall you neap.
O, the roughty old rappe! Minxing marrage
and making loof. Reeve Gootch was right and
Reeve Drughad was sinistrous! And the cut
of him! And the strut of him! How he used to
hold his head as high as a howeth, the famous
eld duke alien, with a hump of grandeur on
him like a walking wiesel rat. And his derry's
own drawl and his corksown blather and his
doubling stutter and his gullaway swank.

Ask Lictor Hackett or Lector Reade of Garda Growley or the Boy with the Billyclub.

miss doddpebble
How elster is he a called at all? Qu'appelle?

missus quickenough
Huges Caput Earlyfouler.

miss doddpebble
Or where was he born or how was he found? Urgothland, Tvistown on the Kattekat? New Hunshire, Concord on the Merrimake? Who blocksmitt her saft anvil or yelled lep to her pail? Was her banns never loosened in Adam and Eve's or were him and her but captain spliced?

missus quickenough
For mine ether duck I thee drake. And by my wildgaze I thee gander. Flowey and Mount on the brink of time makes wishes and fears for a happy isthmass. She can show all her lines, with love, license to play. And if they don't remarry that hook and eye may! O, passmore that and oxus another! Don Dom Dombdomb and his wee follyo!

miss doddpebble
> Was his help inshored in the Stork and
> Pelican against bungelars, flu and third
> risk par-ties? I heard he dug good tin with
> his doll, delvan first and duvlin after, when
> he raped her home, Sabrine asthore, in a
> parakeet's cage, by dredgerous lands and
> devious delts, playing catched and mythed
> with the gleam of her shadda, (if a flic had
> been there to pop up and pepper him!)
> past auld min's manse and Maisons Allfou
> and the rest of incurables and the last of
> immurables, the quaggy waag for stumbling.

- missus quickenough
> Who sold you that jackalantern's tale?
> Pemmican's pasty pie! Not a grasshoop
> to ring her, not an antsgrain of ore. In a
> gabbard he barqued it, the boat of life, from
> the harbourless Ivernikan Okean, till he
> spied the loom of his landfall and he loosed
> two croakers from under his tilt, the gran
> Phenician rover. By the smell of her kelp they
> made the pigeonhouse. Like fun they did!

miss doddpebble
> But where was Himself, the timoneer?

- missus quickenough

    That marchantman he suivied their scutties right over the wash, his cameleer's burnous breezing up on him, till with his runagate bowmpriss he roade and borst her bar. Pilcomayo! Suchcaughtawan! And the whale's away with the grayling! Tune your pipes and fall ahumming, you born ijypt, and you're no-thing short of one!

    miss doddpebble

    Well, ptellomey soon and curb your escumo.

- missus quickenough

    When they saw him shoot swift up her sheba sheath, like any gay lord salomon, her bulls they were ruhring, surfed with spree. Boyarka buah! Boyana bueh! He erned his lille Bunbath hard, our staly bred, the trader. He did. Look at here. In this wet of his prow. Don't you know he was kaldt a bairn of the brine, Wasserbourne the waterbaby? Havemmarea, so he was! Humphrey Chimpden Earwicker has a codfisckee. Shyr she's nearly as badher as him herself.

    miss doddpebble
    Who? Anna Livia?

- missus quickenough
    Ay, Anna Livia.

scene 2

- anna livia plurabelle

    Once it happened, so it may again. Why I'm all these years within years in soffran, allbeleaved. To hide away the tear, the parted. It's thinking of all. The brave that gave their. The fair that wore. All them that's gunne. I'll begin again in a jiffey. The nik of a nad. How glad you'll be I waked you! My! How well you'll feel! For ever after. First we turn by the vagurin here and then it's gooder. So side by side, turn agate, weddingtown, laud men of Londub! I only hope whole the heavens sees us. For I feel I could near to faint away. Into the deeps. Annamores leep. Let me lean, just a lea, if you le, bowldstrong bigtider. Allgearls is wea. At times. So. While you're adamant evar. Wrhps, that wind as if out of norewere! As on the night of the Apophanypes. Jumpst shootst throbbst into me mouth like a bogue and arrohs! Ludegude of the Lashlanns, how he whips me cheeks! Sea, sea! Here, weir, reach, island, bridge. Where you meet I. The day. Remember! Why there that moment and us two only? I was but teen, a tiler's dot. The swankysuits was boosting always, sure him, he was like to me fad. But the swaggerest swell off Shackvulle Strutt. And the fiercest freaky ever followed a pining child round the sluppery table with a forkful of fat. But a king of whistlers. Scieoula! When

he'd prop me atlas against his goose and light
our two candles for our singers duohs on the
sewingmachine. I'm sure he squirted juice in his
eyes to make them flash for flightening me. Still
and all he was awful fond to me. Who'll search
for Find Me Colours now on the hillydroops
of Vikloefells? But I read in Tobecontinued's
tale that while blubles blows there'll still be
sealskers. There'll be others but non so for me.
Yed he never knew we seen us before. Night
after night. So that I longed to go to. And still
withall. One time you'd stand fornenst me,
fairly laughing, in your bark and tan billows
of branches for to fan me coolly. And I'd lie as
quiet as a moss. And one time you'd rush upon
me, darkly roaring, like a great black shadow
with a sheeny stare to perce me rawly. And I'd
frozen up and pray for thawe. Three times in
all. I was the pet of everyone then. A princeable
girl. And you were the pantymammy's Vulking
Corsergoth. The invision of Indelond. And, by
Thorror, you looked it! My lips went livid for
from the joy of fear. Like almost now. How?
How you said how you'd give me the keys of
me heart. And we'd be married till delth to
uspart. And though dev do espart. O mine!
Only, no, now it's me who's got to give. As duv
herself div. Inn this linn. And can it be it's nnow
fforvell? Illas! I wisht I had better glances to
peer to you through this baylight's growing. But
you're changing, acoolsha, you're changing

from me, I can feel. Or is it me is? I'm getting mixed. Brightening up and tightening down. Yes, you're changing, sonhusband, and you're turning, I can feel you, for a daughterwife from the hills again. Imlamaya. And she is coming. Swimming in my hindmoist. Diveltaking on me tail. Just a whisk brisk sly spry spink spank sprint of a thing theresomere, saultering. Saltarella come to her own. I pity your oldself I was used to. Now a Miss Doddpebble's there. Try not to part! Be happy, dear ones! May I be wrong! For she'll be sweet for you as I was sweet when I came down out of me mother. My great blue bedroom, the air so quiet, scarce a cloud. In peace and silence. I could have stayed up there for always only. It's something fails us. First we feel. Then we fall. And let her rain now if she likes. Gently or strongly if she likes.

scene 3

- izzy earwicker

    The cast was thus: see under the clock. Ladies circle: cloaks may be left. Pit, prommer and parterre, standing room only. Habituels conspicuously emergent. A baser meaning has been read into these characters the literal sense of which decency can safely scarcely hint. It has been blurtingly bruited by certain wisecrackers (the stinks of Mohorat are in the nightplots of the morning), that he suffered from a vile disease.

- humphrey chimpden earwicker

    Athma, unmanner them!

- izzy earwicker

    To such a suggestion the one selfrespecting answer is to affirm that there are certain statements which ought not to be, and one should like to hope to be able to add, ought not to be allowed to be made. Nor have his detractors, who, an imperfectly warmblooded race, apparently conceive him as a great white caterpillar capable of any and every enormity in the calendar recorded to the discredit of the Juke and Kellikek families, mended their case by insinuating that, alternately, he lay at one time under the ludicrous imputation of annoying Welsh fusiliers in the people's park.

- humphrey chimpden earwicker
  Hay, hay, hay! Hoq, hoq, hoq! Faun and Flora on the lea love that little old joq. To anyone who knew and loved the christlikeness of the big cleanminded giant H. C. Earwicker throughout his excellency long vicefreegal existence the mere suggestion of him as a lustsleuth nosing for trou-ble in a boobytrap rings particularly preposterous. Truth, beard on prophet, compels one to add that there is said to have been quondam

- izzy earwicker
  (pfuit! pfuit!)

- humphrey chimpden earwicker
  Some case of the kind implicating, it is interdum believed, a quidam

- izzy earwicker
  (if he did not exist it would be necessary quoniam to invent him)

- humphrey chimpden earwicker
    Abhout that time stambuling ha-round
    Dumbaling in leaky sneakers with his tarrk
    record who has remained topantically
    anonymos but ...was, it is stated, posted at
    Mallon's at the instance of watch warriors
    of the vigilance committee and years
    afterwards, cries one even greater, Ibid, a
    commender of the frightful, seemingly, unto
    such as were sulhan sated, tropped head

- izzy earwicker
    (pfiat! pfiat!)

- humphrey chimpden earwicker
    waiting his first of the month froods turn
    for thatt chopp pah kabbakks alicubi
    on the old house for the chargehard,
    Roche Haddocks off Hawkins Street.

- izzy earwicker
    Lowe, you blondy liar, Gob scene you in the
    narked place and she what's edith ar home
    defileth these boyles! There's a cabful of
    bash indeed in the homeur of that meal.

- humphrey chimpden earwicker
    Slander, let it lie its flattest, has never been
    able to convict our good and great and no
    ordinary Southron Earwicker, that homogenius

▸

man, as a pious author called him, of any graver impropriety than that, advanced by some woodwards or regarders, who did not dare deny, the shomers, ...that day consumed their soul of the corn, of having behaved with ongentilmensky immodus opposite a pair of dainty maidservants in the swoolth of the rushy hollow whither, or so the two gown and pinners pleaded, dame nature in all innocency had spontaneously and about the same hour of the eventide sent them both but whose published combinations of silkinlaine testimonies are, where not dubiously pure, visibly divergent, as wapt from wept, on minor points touch- which was admittedly an incautious but, at its wildest, a partial ex – ing the intimate nature of this, a first offence in vert or venison posure with such attenuating circumstances ... as an abnormal Saint Swithin's summer and, ...a ripe occasion to provoke it. We can't do without them. Wives, rush to the restyours!
... If she's a lilyth, pull early! Pauline, allow! And malers abused, keep black, keep black!

- izzy earwicker

Guiltless of much laid to him he was clearly for once at least he clearly expressed himself as being with still a trace of his erstwhile burr sod hence it has been received of us that it is true. They tell the story... how one happygogusty

Ides-of-April morning (the anniversary, as it fell out, of his first assumption of his mirthday suit and rights in appurtenance to the confusioning of human races) ages and ages after the

- humphrey chimpden earwicker
  alleged

- izzy earwicker
  misdemeanour when the tried friend of all creation, tigerwood roadstaff to his stay, was billowing across the wide expanse of our greatest park ... he met a cad with a pipe. The latter, the luciferant not the oriuolate ... to ask could he tell him how much a clock it was that the clock struck had he any idea by cock's luck as his watch was bradys. Hesitency was clearly to be evitated. Execration as cleverly to be honnisoid. The Earwicker of that spurring instant, realising on fundamental liberal principles the supreme importance, nexally and noxally, of physical life (the nearest help relay being pingping K. O. Sempatrick's Day and the fenian rising) and unwishful as he felt of being hurled into eternity right then, plugged by a softnosed bullet from the sap, halted, quick on the draw, and reply ....told the inquiring kidder, by Jehova, it was twelve of em sidereal and tankard time, adding, buttall, as he bended deeply with smoked

▸
sardinish breath to give more pondus to the
copperstick he presented (though this seems
in some cumfusium with the chap ... – as the
hakusay accusation againstm had been made,
what was known in high quarters as was stood
stated in Morganspost, by a creature in youman
form who was quite beneath parr and several
degrees lower than yore triplehydrad snake. ...

- humphrey chimpden earwicker
  Shsh shake, co-comeraid! Me only, them five
  ones, he is equal combat. I have won straight.
  Hence my nonation wide hotel and creamery
  establishments which for the honours of our
  mewmew mutual daughters, credit me, I
  am woo-woo willing to take my stand, sir,
  upon the monument, that sign of our ruru
  redemption, any hygienic day to this hour
  and to make my hoath to my sinnfinners,
  even if I get life for it, upon the Open Bible
  and before the Great Taskmaster's (I lift my
  hat!) and in the presence of the Deity Itself
  andwell of Bishop and Mrs Michan of High
  Church of England as of all such of said my
  immediate withdwellers and of every living
  sohole in every corner wheresoever of this
  globe in general which useth of my British to
  my backbone tongue and commutative justice
  that there is not one tittle of truth, allow me to
  tell you, in that purest of fibfib fabrications.

scene 4

- shem the penman

    Shem is as short for Shemus as
    Jem is joky for Jacob.

- shaun the postman

    A few toughnecks are still getatable
    who pretend that aboriginally he was of
    respectable stemming ... but every honest
    to goodness man in the land of the space of
    today knows that his back life will not stand
    being written about in black and white.

- shem the penman

    Putting truth and untruth together a
    shot may be made at what this hybrid
    actually was like to look at.

- shaun the postman

    Shem's bodily getup, it seems, included an adze
    of a skull, an eight of a larkseye, the whoel of
    a nose, one numb arm up a sleeve, fortytwo
    hairs off his uncrown, eighteen to his mock
    lip, a trio of barbels from his megageg chin
    (sowman's son), the wrong shoulder higher than
    the right, all ears, an artificial tongue with a
    natural curl, not a foot to stand on, a handful of
    thumbs, a blind stomach, a deaf heart, a loose

liver, two fifths of two buttocks, one gleetsteen avoirdupoider for him, a manroot of all evil, a salmonkelt's thinskin, eelsblood in his-cold toes, a bladder tristended, so much so that young Master Shemmy on his very first debouch at the very dawn of protohistory seeing himself such and such, when playing with thistlewords in their garden nursery, Griefotrofio, at Phig Streat III Shuvlin, Old Hoeland, (would we go back there now for sounds, pillings and sense?

- shem the penman
    would we now for annas and annas?

- shaun the postman
    would we for full-score eight and a liretta?

- shem the penman
    for twelve blocks one bob?

- shaun the postman
    for four tes-ters one groat?

- shem the penman
    not for a dinar! not for jo!)

- shaun the postman
    dictited to of all his little brothron and
    sweestureens the first riddle of the universe

- shem the penman
    asking, when is a man not a man?

- shaun the postman
    telling them take their time, yungfries,
    and wait till the tide stops (for from the
    first his day was a fortnight) and offering
    the prize of a bittersweet crab, a little
    present from the past, for their copper
    age was yet unminted, to the winner.

- shem the penman
    One said when the heavens are quakers, a
    second said when Bohemeand lips, a third said
    when he, no, when hold hard a jiffy, when he
    is a gnawstick and detarmined to, the next one
    said when the angel of death kicks the bucket
    of life, still another said when the wine's at
    witsends, and still another when lovely wooman
    stoops to conk him, one of the littliest said me,
    me, Sem, when pappa papared the harbour,
    one of the wittiest said, when he yeat ye
    abblokooken and he zmear hezelf zo zhooken,
    still one said when you are old I'm grey fall full
    wi sleep, and still another when wee deader
    walkner, and another when he is just only after

▶
having being semisized, an-other when yea, he hath no mananas, and one when dose pigs they begin now that they will flies up intil the looft.

- shaun the postman
    All were wrong, so Shem himself, the doctator, took the cake, the correct solution being...

- shem the penman
    ...all give it up?

- shaun the postman
    ...when he is a ...

- shem the penman
    ....yours till the rending of the rocks,

- shaun the postman
    ...Sham.

scene 5

miss doddpebble
> Waiwhou was the first thur- ever burst?

• missus quickenough
> Someone he was, whuebra they were, in a tactic attack or in single combat. Tinker, tilar, souldrer, salor, Pieman Peace or Polistaman. That's the thing I'm elwys on edge to esk. Push up and push vardar and come to uphill headquarters!

miss doddpebble
> Was it waterlows year, after Grattan or Flood, or when maids were in Arc or when three stood hosting?

• missus quickenough
> Fidaris will find where the Doubt arises like Nieman from Nirgends found the Nihil.

miss doddpebble
> Worry you sighin foh, Albern, O Anser? Untie the gemman's fistiknots, Qvic and Nuancee!

- missus quickenough

    She can't put her hand on him for the moment. Tez thelon langlo, walking weary! Such a loon waybash- wards to row! She sid herself she hardly knows whuon the annals her graveller was, a dynast of Leinster, a wolf of the sea, or what he did or how blyth she played or how, when, why, where and who offon he jumpnad her and how it was gave her away. She was just a young thin pale soft shy slim slip of a thing then, sauntering, by silvamoonlake and he was a heavy trudging lurching lieabroad of a Curraghman, making his hay for whose sun to shine on, as tough as the oaktrees (peats be with them!) used to rustle that time down by the dykes of killing Kildare, for forstfellfoss with a plash across her. She thought she's sankh neathe the ground with nymphant shame when he gave her the tigris eye!

miss doddpebble

    O happy fault! Me wish it was he! You're wrong there, corribly wrong! Tisn't only tonight you're anacheronistic! It was ages behind that when nullahs were nowhere, in county Wickenlow, garden of Erin, before she ever dreamt she'd lave Kilbride and go foaming under Horsepass bridge, with the great southwestern windstorming her traces and the midland's grain- waster asarch for her track, to wend her ways byandby, robecca or worse,

to spin and to grind, to swab and to thrash,
for all her golden lifey in the barleyfields and
pennylotts of Humphrey's fordofhurdlestown
and lie with a landleaper, wellingtonorseher.
Alesse, the lagos of girly days!

- missus quickenough

    For the dove of the dunas! Was- ut? Izod?
    Are you sarthin suir? Not where the Finn fits
    into the Mourne, not where the Nore takes
    lieve of Bloem, not where the Braye divarts
    the Farer, not where the Moy changez her
    minds twixt Cullin and Conn tween Cunn
    and Collin? Or where Neptune sculled and
    Tritonville rowed and leandros three bumped
    heroines two? Neya, narev, nen, nonni, nos!

- miss doddpebble

    Then whereabouts in Ow and Ovoca?
    Was it yst with wyst or Lucan Yokan or
    where the hand of man has never set foot?
    Dell me where, the fairy ferse time!

- missus quickenough

    I will if you listen. You know the dinkel dale
    of Luggelaw? Well, there once dwelt a local
    heremite, Michael Arklow was his river- end
    name, (with many a sigh I aspersed his
    lavabibs!) and one venersderg in junojuly, oso

sweet and so cool and so limber she looked,
Nance the Nixie, Nanon L'Escaut, in the silence,
of the sy- comores, all listening, the kindling
curves you simply can't stop feeling, he plunged
both of his newly anointed hands, the core of
his cushlas, in her singimari saffron strumans
of hair, parting them and soothing her and
mingling it, that was deepdark and ample like
this red bog at sundown.... He cuddle not help
himself, thurso that hot on him, he had to
forget the monk in the man so, rubbing her up
and smoothing her down, he baised his lippes
in smiling mood, kiss akiss after kisokushk
(as he warned her niver to, niver to, nevar) on
Anna-na-Poghue's of the freckled forehead.
While you'd parse secheressa she hielt her
souff. But she ruz two feet hire in her aisne
aestumation. And steppes on stilts ever since.
That was kissuahealing with bantur for balm!

miss doddpebble

O, wasn't he the bold priest? And
wasn't she the naughty Livvy?

scene 6

- shem the penman

    Shem was a sham and a low sham and his lowness creeped out first via foodstuffs.

- shaun the postman

    So low was he that he preferred Gibsen's tea-time salmon tinned, as inexpensive as pleasing, to the plumpest roeheavy lax or the friskiest parr or smolt troutlet that ever was gaffed between Leixlip and Island Bridge and many was the time he repeated in his botulism that no junglegrown pineapple ever smacked like the whoppers you shook out of Ananias' cans, Findlater and Gladstone's, Corner House, Englend.

- shem the penman

    None of your inchthick blueblooded Balaclava fried-at-belief-stakes or juicejelly legs of the Grex's molten mutton or greasilygristly grunters' goupons or slice upon slab of luscious goosebosom with lump after load of plumpudding stuffing all aswim in a swamp of bogoakgravy for that greekenhearted yude! Rosbif of Old Zealand! he could not attouch it.

- shaun the postman
    See what happens when your somatophage
    merman takes his fancy to our virgitarian swan?

- shem the penman
    He even ran away with hunself and became
    a farsoonerite, saying he would far sooner
    muddle through the hash of lentils in Europe
    than meddle with Irrland's split little pea.

- shaun the postman
    Once when among those rebels in a state
    of hopelessly helpless intoxication the
    piscivore strove to lift a czitround peel
    to either nostril, hic-cupping, apparently
    impromptued by the hibat he had with his
    glottal stop, that he kukkakould flowrish
    for ever by the smell, as the czitr, as the
    kcedron, like a scedar, of the founts, on
    moun-tains, with limon on, of Lebanon.

- shem the penman
    O! the lowness of him was beneath
    all up to that sunk to!

- shaun the postman
    No likedbylike firewater or first-
    served firstshot or gulletburn gin or
    honest brewbarrett beer either.

- shem the penman
  O dear no!

- shaun the postman
  Instead the tragic jester sobbed himself wheywhing-ingly sick of life on some sort of a rhubarbarous maundarin yella – green funkleblue windigut diodying applejack squeezed from sour grapefruice and, to hear him twixt his sedimental cupslips when he had gulfed down mmmmuch too mmmmany gourds of it retching off to almost as low withswillers, who always knew notwithstanding when they had had enough and were rightly indignant at the wretch's hospitality when they found to their horror they could not carry another drop, it came straight from the noble white fat,...

- shem the penman
  jo,...

- shaun the postman
  openwide sat,

- shem the penman
  jo, jo,...

- shaun the postman
  her why hide that,

- shem the penman
    jo jo jo,...

- shaun the postman
    the winevat, of the most serene magyansty az archdio-chesse, if she is a duck, she's a douches, and when she has a feherbour snot her fault, now is it? artstouchups, funny you're grinning at, fancy you're in her yet, Fanny Urinia.

- shem the penman
    Aint that swell, hey?

- shaun the postman
    Peamengro!

- shem the penman
    Talk about lowness!

scene 7

- missus quickenough

    Nautic Naama's now her navn. Two lads in scoutsch breeches went through her before that, Barefoot Burn and Wallowme Wade, Lugnaquillia's noblesse pickts, before she had a hint of a hair at her fanny to hide or a bossom to tempt a birch canoedler not to mention a bulgic porterhouse barge. And ere that again, leada, laida, all unraidy, too faint to buoy the fairiest rider, too frail to flirt with a cygnet's plume, she was licked by a hound, Chirripa-Chirruta, while poing her pee, pure and simple, on the spur of the hill in old Kippure, in birdsong and shearingtime, but first of all, worst of all, the wiggly livvly, she sideslipped out by a gap in the Devil's glen while Sally her nurse was sound asleep in a sloot and, feefee fiefie, fell over a spillway before she found her stride and lay and wriggled in all the stagnant black pools of rainy under a fallow coo and she laughed innocefree with her limbs aloft and a whole drove of maiden hawthorns blushing and looking askance upon her.

- miss doddpebble

    Drop me the sound of the findhorn's name, Mtu or Mti, som- bogger was wisness. And drip me why in the flenders was she frickled. And

trickle me through was she marcellewaved
or was it weirdly a wig she wore. And
whitside did they droop their glows in their
florry, aback to wist or affront to sea?

- missus quickenough
    In fear to hear the dear so near or
    longing loth and loathing longing? Are
    you in the swim or are you out?

- miss doddpebble
    O go in, go on, go an! I mean
    about what you know.

- missus quickenough
    I know right well what you mean. Rother! You'd
    like the coifs and guimpes, snouty, and me to
    do the greasy jub on old Veronica's wipers.

- miss doddpebble
    What am I rancing now and I'll thank
    you? Is it a pinny or is it a surplice?

- missus quickenough
    Arran, where's your nose?

- miss doddpebble
    And where's the starch?

- missus quickenough

    That's not the vesdre bene- diction smell. I can tell from here by their eau de Colo and the scent of her oder they're Mrs Magrath's. And you ought to have aird them. They've moist come off her. Creases in silk they are, not crampton lawn. Baptiste me, father, for she has sinned! Through her catchment ring she freed them easy, with her hips' hurrahs for her knees'dontelleries. The only parr with frills in old the plain.

miss doddpebble

    So they are, I declare!

- missus quickenough

    Welland well! If tomorrow keeps fine who'll come tripping to sightsee?

miss doddpebble

    How'll?

- missus quickenough

    Ask me next what I haven't got! The Belvedarean exhibitioners. In their cruisery caps and oarsclub colours. What hoo, they band! And what hoa, they buck! And here is her nubilee letters too. Ellis on quay in scarlet thread. Linked for the world on a flush- caloured field. Annan exe after to show they're not Laura Ke- own's. O, may

▶

    the diabolo twisk your seifety pin! You child of Mammon, Kinsella's Lilith! Now who has been tearing the leg of her drawars on her?

- miss doddpebble
   Which leg is it?

- missus quickenough
   The one with the bells on it. Rinse them out and aston along with you! Where did I stop?

- miss doddpebble
   Never stop! Continuarration! You're not there yet. I amstel waiting. Garonne, garonne!

scene 8

- shaun the postman

    Shem, you are. Sh! You are mad!

- shem the penman

    He points the deathbone and the quick are still. Insomnia, somnia somniorum. Awmawm.

- shaun the postman

    MERCIUS (of hisself): Domine vopiscus! My fault, his fault, a kingship through a fault! Pariah, cannibal Cain, I who oathily forswore the womb that bore you and the paps I sometimes sucked, you who ever since have been one black mass of jigs and jimjams, haunted by a convulsionary sense of not having been or being all that I might have been or you meant to becoming, bewailing like a man that innocence which I could not defend...

- shem the penman

    like a woman,...

- shaun the postman

    lo, you there, Cathmon-Carbery, and thank Movies from the innermost depths of my still attrite heart, Wherein the days of youyouth are evermixed mimine, now ere the comp-line

hour of being alone athands itself and a puff
or so before we yield our spiritus to the wind,
for (though that royal one has not yet drunk
a gouttelette from his consummation and the
flowerpot on the pole, the spaniel pack and
their quarry, retainers and the public house
proprietor have not budged a millimetre and
all that has been done has yet to be done and
done again, when's day's woe, and lo, you're
doomed, joyday dawns and, la, you dominate)
it is to you, firstborn and firstfruit of woe,...

- shem the penman
    to me, branded sheep,...

- shaun the postman
    pick of the wasterpaperbaskel, by the
    tremours of Thundery and Ulerin's
    dogstar, you alone, wind-blasted tree of
    the knowledge of beautiful andevil,...

- shem the penman
    ay, clothed upon with the metuor
    and shimmering like the horescens,
    astroglodynamonologos, the child of Nilfit's
    father, blzb, to me unseen blusher in an
    obscene coalhole, the cubilibum of your
    secret sigh, dweller in the downandoutermost
    where voice only of the dead may come,...

- anna livia plurabelle
    …because ye left from me,
    because ye laughed on me,
    because, O me lonly son, ye
    are forgetting me!,…

- shem the penman
    …that our turfbrown mummy is acoming,
    alpilla, beltilla, ciltilla, deltilla, running with
    her tidings, old the news of the great big
    world, sonnies had a scrap, woewoewoe! bab's
    baby walks atseven months, waywayway!

- anna livia plurabelle
    bride leaves her raid at Punchestime, stud
    stoned before a racecourseful, two belles that
    make the one appeal, dry yanks will visit old
    sod, and fourtiered skirts are up, mesdames,
    while Parimiknie wears popular short legs,
    and twelve hows to mix a tipsy wake, did ye
    hear, colt Cooney? did ye ever, filly Fortescue?

- shem the penman
    with a beck, with a spring, all her rillringlets
    shaking, rocks drops in her tachie, tramtokens
    in her hair, all waived to a point and then
    all inuendation, little oldfashioned mummy,
    little wonderful mummy, ducking under

bridges, bellhopping the weirs, dodging by a bit of bog, rapid-shooting round the bends, by Tallaght's green hills and the pools of the phooka and a place they call it Blessington...

- shaun the postman
    and slipping sly by Sallynoggin,

- anna livia plurabelle
    as happy as the day is wet, bab-bling, bubbling,

- shem the penman
    chattering to herself, deloothering the fields on their elbows leaning with the sloothering slide of her,

- anna livia plurabelle
    ...giddy-gaddy, grannyma,

- shem the penman
    gossipaceous Anna Livia.

- shaun the postman
    He lifts the lifewand and the dumb speak.

- anna livia plurabelle
    – Quoiquoiquoiquoiquoiquoiquoiq!

scene 9

- izzy earwicker

    Three quarks for Muster Mark!

    Sure he hasn't got much of a bark

    And sure any he has it's all beside the mark.

    But O, Wreneagle Almighty,
    wouldn't un be a sky of a lark

    To see that old buzzard whooping
    about for uns shirt in the dark

    And he hunting round for uns speckled
    trousers around by Palmer-stown Park?

    Hohohoho, moulty Mark!

    You're the rummest old rooster ever
    flopped out of a Noah's ark

    And you think you're cock of the wark.

    Fowls, up! Tristy's the spry young spark

    That'll tread her and wed her
    and bed her and red her

    Without ever winking the tail of a feather

    And that's how that chap's going to
    make his money and mark!

- humphrey chimpden earwicker
  Overhoved, shrillgleescreaming. That song sang seaswans. The winging ones. Seahawk, seagull, curlew and plover, kestrel and capercallzie. All the birds of the sea they trolled out rightbold when they smacked the big kuss of Trustan with Usolde.

- izzy earwicker
  And there they were too, when it was dark, whilest the wild-caps was circling, as slow their ship, the winds aslight, upborne the fates, the wardorse moved, by courtesy of Mr Deaubaleau Downbellow Kaempersally, listening in, as hard as they could, in Dubbeldorp, the donker, by the tourneyold of the wattarfalls, with their vuoxens and they kemin in so hattajocky (only a quartebuck askull for the last acts) to the solans and the sycamores and the wild geese and the gannets and the migratories and the mistlethrushes and the auspices and all the birds of the rockby-suckerassousyoceanal sea, all four of them, all sighing and sob – bing, and listening. Moykle ahoykling!

- humphrey chimpden earwicker
  They were the big four, the four maaster waves of Erin, all listening, four. There was old Matt Gregory and then besides old Matt there was old Marcus Lyons, the four waves, and oftentimes they used to be saying grace

▸

together, right enough, bausnabeatha, in
Miracle Squeer: here now we are the four of
us: old Matt Gre-gory and old Marcus and
old Luke Tarpey: the four of us and sure,
thank God, there are no more of us: and,
sure now, you wouldn't go and forget and
leave out the other fellow and old Johnny
MacDougall: the four of us and no more of
us and so now pass the fish for Christ sake,
Amen: the way they used to be saying their
grace before fish, repeating itself, after the
interims of Augusburgh for auld lang syne.

- izzy earwicker

    And so there they were, with their
    palms in their hands, like the pulchrum's
    proculs, spraining their ears, luistening
    and listening to the oceans of kissening,
    with their eyes glistening, all the four,

- humphrey chimpden earwicker

    when he was kiddling and cuddling
    and bunnyhugging scrumptious his
    colleen bawn and dinkum belle, an
    oscar sister, on the fifteen inch loveseat,
    behind the chieftaness stewardesses
    cubin, the hero, of Gaelic champion,

- izzy earwicker

    the onliest one of her choice, her bleaueyedeal
    of a girl's friend, neither bigugly nor smallnice,
    meaning pretty much everything to her
    then, with his sinister dexterity, light and
    rufthandling, vicemversem her ragbags et
    assaucyetiams, fore and aft, on and offsides, the
    brueburnt sexfutter, handson and huntsem, that
    was palpably wrong and bulbubly improper,
    and cuddling her and kissing her, tootyfay
    charmaunt, in her ensemble of maidenna blue,
    with an overdress of net, tickled with goldies,
    Isolamisola, and whisping and lisping her about
    Trisolanisans, how one was whips for one was
    two and two was lips for one was three, and
    dissimulating themself, with his poghue like
    Arrah-na-poghue, the dear dear annual, they
    all four remembored who made the world
    and how they used to be at that time in the
    vulgar ear cuddling and kiddling her, after
    an oyster supper in Cullen's bam, from under
    her mistlethrush and kissing and listening,

- humphrey chimpden earwicker

    in the good old bygone days of Dion Boucicault,
    the elder, in Arrah-na-pogue, in the otherworld
    of the passing of the key of Two – tongue
    Common, with Nush, the carrier of the word,
    and with Mesh, the cutter of the reed, in one
    of the farback, pitchblack centuries when who
    made the world, when they knew O'Clery,

▸ the man on the door, when they were all four
collegians on the nod, neer the Nodderlands
Nurskery, whiteboys and oakboys, peep of tim
boys and piping tom boys, raising hell while
the sin was shining, with their slates and
satchels, playing Florian's fables and communic
suctions and vellicar frictions with mixum
mem-bers, in the Queen's Ultonian colleges,
along with another fellow, a prime number,
Totius Quotius, and paying a pot of tribluts
to Boris O'Brien, the buttler of Clumpthump,
two looves, two turnovers plus (one) crown,
to see the mad dane ating his vitals.

- izzy earwicker

    Wulf! Wulf! And throwing his tongue
    in the snakepit. Ah ho! The ladies have
    mercias! It brought the dear prehistoric
    scenes all back again, as fresh as of yore,
    Matt and Marcus, natu-ral born lovers of
    nature, in all her moves and senses,

- humphrey chimpden earwicker

    and after that now there he was, that
    mouth of mandibles, vowed to pure
    beauty, and his Arrah-na-poghue,

- izzy earwicker
    when she murmurously, after she let
    a cough, gave her firm order,

- humphrey chimpden earwicker
    if he wouldn't please mind, for a sings to one
    hope a dozen of the best favourite lyrical
    national blooms in Luvillicit, though not too
    much, reflecting on the situation, drinking in
    draughts of purest air serene and re-velling in
    the great outdoors, before the four of them,
    in the fair fine night, whilst the stars shine
    bright, by she light of he moon, we longed
    to be spoon, before her honeyoldloom, the
    plaint effect being in point of fact there
    being in the whole, a seatuition so shocking
    and scandalous and now, thank God, there
    were no more of them and he poghuing
    and poghuing like the Moreigner bowed his
    crusted hoed and Tilly the Tailor's Tugged a
    Tar in the Arctic Newses Dagsdogs number
    and there they were, like a foremasters in the
    rolls, listening, to Rolando's deepen darblun
    Ossian roll, (Lady, it was just too gorgeous,
    that expense of a lovely tint, embellished by
    the charms of art and very well conducted
    and nicely mannered and all the horrid rudy
    noisies locked up in nasty cubbyhole!)

- izzy earwicker

   as tired as they were, the three jolly topers, with their mouths watering, all the four, the old connu-bial men of the sea, yambing around with their old pantometer, in duckasaloppics, Luke and Johnny MacDougall and all wishening for anything at all of the bygone times, the wald times and the fald times and the hempty times and the dempty times, for a cup of kindness yet, for four farback tumblerfuls of woman squash, with them, all four, listening and spraining their ears for the millennium and all their mouths making water.

scene 10

- anna livia plurabelle

  Anyway let her rain for my time is come. I done me best when I was let. Thinking always if I go all goes. A hundred cares, a tithe of troubles and is there one who understands me? One in a thousand of years of the nights? All me life I have been lived among them but now they are becoming lothed to me. And I am lothing their little warm tricks. And lothing their mean cosy turns. And all the greedy gushes out through their small souls. And all the lazy leaks down over their brash bodies. How small it's all! And me letting on to meself always. And lilting on all the time. I thought you were all glittering with the noblest of carriage. You're only a bumpkin. I thought you the great in all things, in guilt and in glory. You're but a puny. Home! My people were not their sort out beyond there so far as I can. For all the bold and bad and bleary they are blamed, the seahags. No! Nor for all our wild dances in all their wild din. I can seen meself among them, allaniuvia pulchrabelled. How she was handsome, the wild Amazia, when she would seize to my other breast! And what is she weird, haughty Niluna, that she will snatch from my ownest hair! For 'tis they are the stormies. Ho hang! Hang ho! And the clash of our cries till we spring to be free. Auravoles, they says, never heed of your name! But I'm loothing them that's here and all I lothe. Loonely in me loneness. For all their faults. I am passing out. O bitter ending! I'll slip away before they're up. They'll never see. Nor know. Nor miss me. And it's old and old it's sad and old it's sad and weary I go back to you, my cold father, my cold mad father, my cold mad feary father, till the near sight of the mere size of him, the moyles and moyles of it, moananoaning, makes me seasilt saltsick and I rush, my only, into your arms. I see them rising! Save me from those therrble prongs! Two more. Onetwo moremens more. So. Avelaval. My leaves have drifted from me. All. But one clings still. I'll bear it on me. To remind me of. Lff! So soft this morning, ours. Yes. Carry me along, taddy, like you done through the toy fair! If I seen him bearing down on me now under whitespread wings like he'd come from Arkangels, I sink I'd die down over his feet, humbly dumbly, only to washup. Yes, tid. There's where. First. We pass through grass behush the bush to. Whish! A gull. Gulls. Far calls. Coming, far! End here. Us then. Finn, again! Take. Bussoftlhee, mememormee! Till thousendsthee. Lps. The keys to. Given! A way a lone a last a loved a long the riverrun, past Eve and Adam's, from swerve of shore to bend of bay, brings us by a commodius vicus of recirculation back to Howth Castle and Environs.

SCENE 11

- missus quickenough

    Well, you know or don't you kennet or haven't I told you every telling has a taling and that's the he and the she of it. Look, look, the dusk is growing! My branches lofty are taking root.

miss doddpebble

    And my cold cher's gone ashley. Fieluhr? Filou! What age is at? It saon is late.

- missus quickenough

    'Tis endless now senne eye or erewone last saw Waterhouse's clogh. They took it asunder, I hurd thum sigh. When will they reassemble it? O, my back, my back, my bach! I'd want to go to Aches-les-Pains. Pingpong! There's the Belle for Sexaloitez! And Concepta de Send-us-pray! Pang! Wring out the clothes! Wring in the dew! Godavari, vert the showers! And grant thaya grace! Aman.

miss doddpebble

    Will we spread them here now?

- missus quickenough

    Ay, we will. Flip! Spread on your bank and I'll spread mine on mine.

miss doddpebble
Flep! It's what I'm doing.

- missus quickenough
Spread! It's churning chill. Der went is rising. I'll lay a few stones on the hostel sheets. A man and his bride embraced between them. Else I'd have sprinkled and folded them only.

miss doddpebble
And I'll tie my butcher's apron here. It's suety yet. The strollers will pass it by. Six shifts, ten kerchiefs, nine to hold to the fire and this for the code, the convent napkins, twelve, one baby's shawl.

- missus quickenough
Good mother Jossiph knows, she said.

miss doddpebble
Whose head? Mutter snores? Deataceas! Wharnow are alle her childer, say? In kingdome gone or power to come or gloria be to them farther? Allalivial, allalluvial!

- missus quickenough
Some here, more no more, more again lost alla stranger. I've heard tell that same brooch of the Shannons was married into a family

in Spain. And all the Dun- ders de Dunnes in Markland's Vineland beyond Brendan's herring pool takes number nine in yangsee's hats. And one of Biddy's beads went bobbing till she rounded up lost histereve with a marigold and a cobbler's candle in a side strain of a main drain of a manzinahurries off Bachelor's Walk. But all that's left to the last of the Meaghers in the loup of the years prefixed and between is one kneebuckle and two hooks in the front.

- miss doddpebble
  Do you tell me that now?

- missus quickenough
  I do in troth.

- miss doddpebble
  Orara por Orbe and poor Las Animas! Ussa, Ulla, we're umbas all!

- missus quickenough
  Mezha, didn't you hear it a deluge of times, ufer and ufer, respund to spond? You deed, you deed!

miss doddpebble
> I need, I need! It's that irrawaddyng
> I've stoke in my aars. It all but husheth
> the lethest zswound. Oronoko!

- missus quickenough
  > What's your trouble?

miss doddpebble
> Is that the great Finnleader himself in his
> joakimono on his statue riding the high horse
> there forehengist? Father of Otters, it is himself!
> Yonne there! Isset that? On Fallareen Common?

- missus quickenough
  > You're thinking of Astley's Amphitheayter where
  > the bobby restrained you making sugarstuck
  > pouts to the ghostwhite horse of the Peppers.
  > Throw the cobwebs from your eyes, woman,
  > and spread your washing proper! It's well I
  > know your sort of slop. Flap! Ireland sober
  > is Ireland stiff. Lord help you, Maria, full of
  > grease, the load is with me! Your prayers.

miss doddpebble
> I sonht zo! Madammangut! Were you
> lifting your elbow, tell us, glazy cheeks,
> in Conway's Carrigacurra canteen?

- missus quickenough

    Was I what, hobbledyhips? Flop! Your rere gait's creakorheuman bitts your butts disagrees. Amn't I up since the damp dawn, marthared mary allacook, with Corri- gan's pulse and varicoarse veins, my pramaxle smashed, Alice Jane in decline and my oneeyed mongrel twice run over, soaking and bleaching boiler rags, and sweating cold, a widow like me, for to deck my tennis champion son, the laundryman with the lavandier flannels?

- miss doddpebble

    You won your limpopo limp fron the husky hussars when Collars and Cuffs was heir to the town and your slur gave the stink to Carlow. Holy Scamander, I sar it again! Near the golden falls. Icis on us! Seints of light! Zezere!

- missus quickenough

    Subdue your noise, you hamble creature! What is it but a blackburry growth or the dwyergray ass them four old codgers owns.

- miss doddpebble

    Are you meanam Tarpey and Lyons and Gregory?

- missus quickenough

    I meyne now, thank all, the four of
    them, and the roar of them, that draves
    that stray in the mist and old Johnny
    MacDougal along with them.

- miss doddpebble

    Is that the Poolbeg flasher beyant, pharphar,
    or a fireboat coasting nyar the Kishtna
    or a glow I behold within a hedge or my
    Garry come back from the Indes?

- missus quickenough

    Wait till the honeying of the lune, love! Die
    eve, little eve, die! We see that wonder in your
    eye. We'll meet again, we'll part once more.

- miss doddpebble

    The spot I'll seek if the hour you'll find.

- missus quickenough

    My chart shines high where the blue milk's
    upset. Forgivemequick, I'm going! Bubye!

- miss doddpebble

    And you, pluck your watch, forgetmenot.
    Your evenlode. So save to jurna's end!

- missus quickenough

    My sights are swimming thicker on
    me by the sha- dows to this place.

miss doddpebble

    I sow home slowly now by own
    way, moy- valley way.

- missus quickenough

    Towy I too, rathmine. Ah, but she was
    the queer old skeowsha anyhow, Anna
    Livia, trinkettoes! And sure he was the
    quare old buntz too, Dear Dirty Dumpling,
    foostherfather of fingalls and dotthergills.
    Gammer and gaffer we're all their gangsters.

miss doddpebble

    Hadn't he seven dams to wive him?

- missus quickenough

    And every dam had her seven crutches. And
    every crutch had its seven hues. And each hue
    had a differing cry. Sudds for me and supper
    for you and the doctor's bill for Joe John.
    Befor! Bifur! He married his markets, cheap
    by foul, I know, like any Etrurian Catholic
    Heathen, in their pinky limony creamy
    birnies and their turkiss indienne mauves.

- miss doddpebble

    But at milkidmass who was the spouse?

- missus quickenough

    Then all that was was fair. Tys Elvenland! Teems of times and happy returns. The seim anew. Ordovico or viricordo. Anna was, Livia is, Plurabelle's to be. Northmen's thing made southfolk's place but howmulty plurators made eachone in per-son? Latin me that, my trinity scholar, out of eure sanscreed into oure eryan! Hircus Civis Eblanensis! He had buckgoat paps on him, soft ones for orphans. Ho, Lord! Twins of his bosom. Lord save us! And ho! Hey? What all men. Hot? His tittering daugh- ters of. Whawk?

- miss doddpebble

    Can't hear with the waters of. The chittering waters of. Flitter- ing bats, fieldmice bawk talk. Ho! Are you not gone ahome?

- missus quickenough

    What Thom Malone?

- miss doddpebble

    Can't hear with bawk of bats, all thim liffey-ing waters of. Ho, talk save us!

- missus quickenough
    My foos won't moos. I feel as old as yonder elm.

miss doddpebble
    A tale told of Shaun or Shem?

- missus quickenough
    All Livia's daughter-sons. Dark hawks hear us. Night! Night! My ho head halls.

miss doddpebble
    I feel as heavy as yonder stone. Tell me of John or Shaun? Who were Shem and Shaun the living sons or daughters of?

- missus quickenough
    Night now!

miss doddpebble
    Tell me, tell me, tell me, elm!

- missus quickenough
    Night night!

miss doddpebble
    Telmetale of stem or stone. Beside the rivering waters of, hitherandthithering waters of.

www.ingramcontent.com/pod-product-compliance
Lightning Source LLC
Chambersburg PA
CBHW071318080526
44587CB00018B/3264